EAGLES IN CHICKEN COOPS

An Identity Theft Crisis

Jay Stewart

Eagles in Chicken Coops
A Identity Theft Crisis
By Jay Stewart

Printed in the United States of America

ISBN 978-1-60266-956-7

www.xulonpress.com

Dedication

This book is dedicated to my wife Melanie, inspiration to many, woman of God, wife, mother, and co-pastor of The Refuge. You have fought a fierce enemy for your identity, and have never looked more like your Father than now! I have always loved you.

To Haley, my daughter. You are such a leader and overcomer. The destiny ahead is massive and you have good reason to smile at your future.

To Clay and Cole, my Irish twins who keep me young, laughing, and learning. You are both such young men of God, and I know you will far exceed your Dad's kingdom accomplishments.

To Caden, my warrior and fighter. You came out swinging, and have been such a source of blessing in your short time on earth.

To the great staff, leaders, and community of believers who make up The Refuge. You are being the church like I have never seen. Thanks for making pastoring such fun.

Endorsements

"Jay Stewart is a prophetic and authentic vessel of grace and vision who is impacting a region. I believe that this book will equip and encourage people to rise up in the Spirit of an overcomer and give them eyes for the snares of the enemy that prevent people from entering their destiny. It doesn't take much to hold one down, if they are not trying to get free or if they are ignorant of the schemes of darkness. After reading this material you will find out what God's original intention is and how to supernaturally morph into the end-time greatness that you are called to become."

Sean Smith
Author of "Prophetic Evangelism"
National Speaker

"It has been such a privilege over the last few years to call this anointed man of God my pastor. The pages of this book contain such a timely word indeed! It's time for the church to stand up and embrace our identity in Christ Jesus, run head-long into our destiny, and in the Spirit, soar like the eagles we were created to be."

Mike Weaver
Recording Artist/Song Writer
Big Daddy Weave

"Jay has not only captured information, but revelation concerning the most important issues of any believer. If you do not allow God's Word to define who you are, other people will not only define you, but classify you, and possibly render you ineffective for your mission in life. The principles set forth in this book are essential for leaders and individuals who want to be effective in the Kingdom of God. You must do more than just read it; you must employ its teachings. This book should be in everyone's library and referred to often."

Bishop Paul D. Zink
Senior Pastor, New Life Christian Fellowship

"*Eagles in Chicken Coops* might be the greatest literary work of our time. Jay Stewart captures and articulates a message that everyone needs to hear. His style of communication is unmatched, brilliant, and even spell-binding. I can honestly say that Jay is one of the greatest, most gifted, talented, and handsome men I have ever had the privilege of meeting. And this book is reflective of those qualities!"

Lynette Stewart
Mother of the Author

"Jay Steweart is far more than a book author. He is my Pastor, my spiritual guide, my counselor and most important to me, my friend. He is a man of great wisdom and insight that extends way beyond his years. There's one thing I know about Jay Stewart—he does nothing without due diligence and everything he does, he does with excellence. You will thoroughly enjoy this read. I am blessed to have him in my life and you, the reader of this book, are now blessed to have him in yours."

Nikita Koloff
Former world-champion wrestler
Evangelist and Author
Koloff for Christ Ministries

"The realization and ascent to one's destiny is a truth that is central to our life's story. This work speaks to this issue deeply and calls for you to "come up higher." There is no place higher than worship! The message here will help unlock your chains and recover what has been stolen from you. Prepare for an "Aha" moment!"

Lindell Cooley
Senior Pastor, Grace Church
Nashville, Tennessee

"The devil knows that your destiny is wrapped up in your identity in Christ. If he can keep you from your identity, he can stop you from fulfilling what God created you for. So many live their lives unfulfilled because they have never found out who they were created to be. Jay Stewart has so exposed the strategy of the enemy and released truths that will cause you to embrace your true identity. This book will cause you to see yourself in light of God's opinion and approval, and release you to your true identity. Read, receive, and soar!"

Rusty Nelson
Pastor
The Rock Family Worship Center
Huntsville, Alabama

Table of Contents

Chapter 1

Fly High

Most human beings have had an "aha" moment, a point in time when they came to the realization, "I don't belong here. I was made for something better than this!" It could have been the result of a summer job, an abusive relationship, or an activity that led to destruction, addiction, or shame. Some people actually take that realization and do something about their situation, bettering their life and becoming the person God intended them to be all along. Others, however, settle for something less than what they were made for.

This is a book about re-discovering your true identity. It is a lingering look into the full-length mirror of self, soul, and God's Word. It is intended to provoke you, rattle you, shake you, and awaken you to your destiny. It presents you with an opportunity to realize that maybe you, like millions of others, have settled for something less than what and who you were created to be.

As children, we dream of one day becoming an astronaut, walking the runway in the Miss America pageant, fighting fires as a fireman, being elected President of the United States, or discovering the cure for cancer. There are dreams as well, which God has put in each person's heart, of being someone or doing something to make a difference in the lives of others—contributing something of eternal value, realizing a destiny and a purpose that was inscribed in your DNA, as much as blue eyes or short legs. Yet from the moment you were conceived, enemies began fighting for that purpose, clawing at your identity and presenting an oftentimes convincing case that those were pie-in-the-sky dreams which would never be reached.

The eagle is the symbol of America, and for good reasons. There is no animal that can match its beauty, strength, grace, majesty, and ability. The eagle sits at the top of the food chain. According to scientists, aerodynamically, it is impossible for the eagle to fly. Yet, it is the greatest flying bird of all. With its 7000 feathers, bald eagles can fly to an altitude of 10,000 feet. During level flight, they can achieve speeds of about 30 to 35 mph. Its hollow bones and 6-8 foot wing span cause it to soar on winds to these great heights, where it builds its nests beyond the reach of other animals. The eagle hunts in an area ranging from 1,700 to 10,000 acres. Its remarkable eyesight makes it possible for it to spot a fish below the surface of the water from hundreds of feet in the air.

The creator of the eagle, who designed this amazing species, also made you. And He created you in His image with the ability to fly high. The greatness of God is resident in you, and His plan for you is that "you will always be at the top, never at the bottom" (Deuteronomy 28:13). David writes in Psalm 103:5 that the Lord "satisfies your desires with good things so that your youth is renewed like the eagle's." We also find written these words in Isaiah 40:31: "...but those who hope in the Lord will renew their strength. They will soar on wings like eagles; they will run and not grow weary, they will walk and not be faint."

My wife and I spent a nice, Carolina-spring morning at the zoo recently with one of our sons on a school field trip. In an enclosure about the size of a small house, an eagle was kept. It had the space to fly a distance of maybe 20-30 feet. How majestic, grand, and powerful the bird looked perched on a limb in the enclosure. I am sure the bird is well taken care of, but it was sad to see this creature of beauty, who is used to flying high for miles, limited to such a small space. Of course a worse scenario for the eagle would have been to be captured by a confused chicken farmer and caged in a chicken coop. Imagine the ridicule, shame, humiliation, embarrassment, and frustration of living a life so far below your potential.

And nothing could be worse than for you to end up settling for something far less than what you were made for. You were created to fly high, so start flapping and catch the wind of His spirit blowing through the pages of this book. Come on.......let's soar!

Chapter 2

Criminal Intent

I walked out of my garage early in the morning for our men's study at a local restaurant, left there an hour later for the gym for a workout, and then headed for the office. Upon answering my cell phone, the first thing my wife said to me was "Where's my van?" "That's funny!" I replied. "What do you mean, 'Where's your van?' I guess it is right there in the driveway." Normally parked in the garage, the van had to spend a couple of nights in the driveway while some furniture occupied its space. "Well, I just walked outside and my van is not there!"

I turned and headed for home, thinking she somehow just overlooked it. But how do you overlook a minivan? The police arrived to fill out the report, and it was easy to discern from the officer that: A. this was routine and mundane to him and B. that he had little optimism about the van ever being seen again. We, like millions of others, were victims of crime, something that occurs everyday.

The fastest growing crime in America, however, has nothing to do with drugs, car theft, or murder. It is identity theft, and the average victim loses $2412. People dig through trash cans looking for discarded credit card statements, bills, or other personal information that can be used to fraudulently "become" another person. They will obtain social security numbers over the phone by promising a check within the next 7 days, and then use the numbers to steal the identity of the naïve, unsuspecting victim. What happens in a matter of a few minutes can take months to correct, cause much anxiety and stress, and create financial hardships that can take years to erase.

As terrible as this is, there is a worse crime occurring everyday that is literally ruining the lives of thousands. A bandit is on the loose, wreaking havoc on the weak, the strong, the old, the young, the wealthy, the poor, the educated, and the uneducated. He is no respecter of persons, he places no value on human life, and he is not content with anything less than total destruction. Satan has long been recognized, even before the foundations of the earth were set, as a thief and a destroyer. And he is after the identity of believers, wanting to rob them of the likeness they bear to the Father.

His intentions are clear and criminal in the worst sense. However, there is One who stands as a defender of the weak, a restorer to the impoverished, a healer to the wounded, a joy-giver to the depressed, a conqueror to the conquered, a singer to the songless, and a life-giver to the lifeless. God himself is fighting for you today. There is nothing you can do that will make Him love you any more, and there is nothing you can do that will make Him love you any less! He looks beyond our marred, disfigured images, and sees the likeness of the One in whose image we were created.

Could it be that you have discovered that something valuable has been stolen from you? Or maybe you've had an "aha" moment, realizing that who you are now is not who you were created to be. Allow yourself to hope again. Imagine yourself soaring high, reaching new heights, fulfilling dreams, discovering purpose and destiny. Together we will investigate and uncover the fraudulent, divisive tactics of the enemy, and allow God to restore us to our original appearance. You are an eagle, and eagles don't belong in chicken coops!

Chapter 3

Has the devil Stolen Your Worship?

When we made our grand, naked entrance into the world, two things were already established. The first was that, instilled in each of us from the moment of birth, was the desire to worship. The reason we have life and language is for worship. We are the only beings out of all creation that can worship with words, and that can choose to worship Him. Birds, trees, grasshoppers, ocean waves, and all other forms of creation do not choose to worship the Messiah. They just do. The sounds they make are worship to Him. We, on the other hand, have a choice. The fact is that everyone will worship something or somebody, but we still must choose the object of our worship.

The second thing that was established from the moment we came into the world was the enemy's goal to steal our worship. Like a ravenous lion on the Serengeti that hasn't eaten in weeks, the devil craves what we possessed from birth.....the desire and capacity to worship. But there is more to it than just that. There is a reason he is so intent on robbing us of our worship. He's after a bigger prize, something more valuable to him than even our worship. Curious?

It all began long before you and I existed. In the vast expanses of heaven's halls, inappropriately interrupting the majestic worship of angels, the angel of light, Lucifer, makes a declaration. "I will ascend to heaven; I will raise my throne above the stars of God; I will sit enthroned on the mount of assembly, on the utmost heights of the sacred mountain. I will ascend above the tops of the clouds; I will make myself like the Most High." (Is. 14:13, 14). Did you catch that last line? "I will make myself like the Most High." He was jealous of God's position, power, and prominence, and plotted to steal from the Most High. What gall! One swift backhand from Elohim and he was cast down to the pit. But he wouldn't stop there. He schemed and conceived Plan B.

There is a great truth about us found in Genesis 1:27. It says that we are created in the image of God. We bear a striking resemblance to the Father when we come into this world. And to the enemy, it's almost as if God is rubbing defeat in satan's face as He freely gives His image to all mankind. Thus Plan B. If he can't have the image of God, satan is determined that you and I won't have it either. When we worship God, we become more like him, and his image is perfected in us. Satan is after the image of God in us.

In Genesis 3:1-5 we read these words: "Now the serpent was more crafty than any of the wild animals the LORD God had made. He said to the woman, "Did God really say, 'You must not eat from any tree in the garden'?" 2 The woman said to the serpent, "We may eat fruit from the trees in the garden, 3 but God did say, 'You must not eat fruit from the tree that is in the middle of the garden, and you must not touch it, or you will die.' " 4 "You will not surely die," the serpent said to the woman. 5 "For God knows that when you eat of it your eyes will be opened, and ***you will be like God*** (emphasis added), knowing good and evil."

How does he steal our identity? He uses things like.....

Shame
Anger
Disappointment
Disobedience
Guilt
Condemnation
Pride and

apathy to keep us from worshipping. And the very thing we need, His presence— the thing that draws us to Him, changes us, refreshes us, and transforms us—becomes the thing that we often lose. This sends us into a cycle of these evils, pushing us further and further from Him. It is a classic case of identity theft, an attempt to rob us of the resemblance we bear to the Father. The simple truth is that the more we worship Him, the more like Him we become, and the more steadfast His image remains in us. The less we worship, the faster His image in us deteriorates. Sin separates us from God, and when the enemy lures us into acts that feed our flesh, we become separated from the Lord. That is when the enemy begins to get up in our head and convince us that we cannot, or should not, approach a holy God through worship. Satan keeps us from the very thing we need, God's presence, which restores us to His image. And the cycle begins. We feel worse about ourselves, which causes more shame, which in turn makes it even more difficult to approach a holy, loving Father, and we plunge deeper into a mistaken and false identity.

The citizens of Feldkirch, Austria, didn't know what to do. Napoleon's massive army was preparing to attack. Soldiers had been spotted on the heights above the little town, which was situated on the Austrian border. A council of citizens was hastily summoned to decide whether they should try to defend themselves or display the white flag of surrender. It happened to be Easter Sunday, and the people had gathered in the local church. The pastor rose and said, "Friends, we have been counting on our own strength, and apparently that has failed. As this is the day of our Lord's resurrection, let us just ring the bells, have our services as usual, and leave the matter in His hands. We know only our weakness, and not the power of God to defend us." The council accepted his plan and the church bells rang. The enemy, hearing the sudden peal, concluded that the Austrian army had arrived during the night to defend the town. Before the service ended, the enemy broke camp and left.

Nothing sets the enemy fleeing like heartfelt declarations of worship. David said, "I lift up my eyes to the hills. Where does my help come from? My help comes from the Lord, the maker of heaven and earth." (Psalm) We were created to worship, so lift up your eyes to Him, lift up your voice to the one you can trust to rescue and send the enemy away. Let it ring out and watch the thief run.

Chapter 4

Truths About Worship

Worship is supernatural. It is an expression of our hearts to a supernatural God, an avenue into His presence that opens up to us a realm that is above the physical, natural realm in which we abide. Defiled worship, however, will take people into a supernatural realm, a realm of darkness, for the sole purpose of then ensnaring them in the realm of the natural. In John 4:24 we read, "God is spirit, and his worshipers must worship in spirit and in truth." Why? In order to remain in the realm of the supernatural, the realm of His kingdom, which is far superior to this natural realm. Speaking of the devil, John writes in John 8:44 that "...there is no truth in him. When he lies, he speaks his native language, for he is a liar and the father of lies." He is the polar opposite of God. He was booted out of the realm that is superior, and now is incapable of speaking truth. So he seeks to defile our worship and disfigure our image so that we will cease to believe the truth, therefore making it impossible for us to worship in truth. He makes attempts to progressively steal our identity as worshippers so that we will, little by little, become increasingly satisfied with the natural, the realm of the enemy.

Do you realize that the only thing we do on Earth, which we will also do in heaven, is to worship? There will be no witnessing in heaven, no capital fundraising, no Bible studies, no outreach programs, no prayer meetings, no healing lines, no missions banquets, and no children's Christmas programs. Tommy Tenney says that worship is the only part of our service that God gets anything out of. He is not moved by our preaching. Can you imagine God elbowing Gabriel during some sermon and saying, "Man, that's good stuff! I didn't know that." Not once has He ever asked for my notes so he could go back and fill in some missing points in his notes. The purpose of preaching is to raise up worshippers. There will be no preaching in heaven, but there will be plenty of worship.

Odds are you have read or heard of the showdown Jesus had with satan in the desert. It is found in Matthew 4:8-11, and says

"8Again, the devil took him to a very high mountain and showed him all the kingdoms of the world and their splendor. 9"All this I will give you," he said, "if you will bow down and worship me." 10Jesus said to him, "Away from me, Satan! For it is written: 'Worship the Lord your God, and serve him only.'" 11Then the devil left him, and angels came and attended him."

Here are some basic truths about worship that will help protect you against becoming a victim of identity theft.

You become like the one you worship. One of the first questions you should ask yourself is this: What or who is the object of my worship? You will take on the characteristics and heart of the one you worship.

The more you worship, the more natural it becomes. To get good at anything you have to do it over and over again. In time, the repeated motion or activity becomes so fluid and natural that you don't even have to think about it. Mike Weaver of the group Big Daddy Weave, says, "Worship is about our entire life response to the greatness and glory of God. We don't have to think about breathing…it just happens. As a worshipper of God, that's the place that I want to learn to live—seeing God in every moment, and learning to respond naturally with my life."

Your feelings will follow your actions. We often look for the easy way in life, and because of that, we want to feel and then act. It makes it much easier to get started on something if you feel like it. Feelings can be a great motivator. However, if every couple waited until they felt like being nice to each other, or being romantic, or putting the other first, the divorce rate would probably be much higher. And in our relationship with Christ, we are often required to act before we feel. But when you act out of obedience to Him, and in response to who He is, the feelings will come.

Worship puts you in a place of authority and rest. Jesus was at the end of forty days of fasting, yet we see in his showdown with satan such authority. David wrote in Psalm 100 that we should, "Enter his gates with thanksgiving and his courts with praise." (vs. 4) The word "gate" means the place of authority. The gates of a city were the place where the authorities sat and decided on various issues. The word "thanksgiving" comes from the Hebrew word "todah", which means the lifting of the hand as in a show of agreement. In a courtroom, a witness is asked to place one hand on the Bible, and to raise the other hand, showing that they will testify truthfully about the facts. When we come into agreement with what God has said, it brings us into His authority. David also said to come into the courts with praise. The court was the place of settlement. The word "praise" comes from the Hebrew word "tehilla", which means "crazy praise". What David is saying here is that when we come into God's authority on a matter, whether it be sickness, finances, children, your business, the state of your marriage, or any other issue, and we agree with God's Word, it brings us into a place where the matter is settled, which then produces in us a crazy praise, or a praise that doesn't make sense to others.

Worship lifts you above the realm of the natural. Again, the goal of the enemy is to keep you in the realm of the natural, and God is always seeking to call us higher. Isaiah said that when we wait on the Lord, He would give us renewed strength that would cause us to soar high above circumstances, problems, pressures, or the snares of the enemy. Worship releases the breath of God beneath your wings!

Worship brings you into intimacy with God. One night stands are cheap, but a long-term marriage is priceless. Worship lifts us higher, but intimacy with God keeps us there. The goal of worship is not to be blessed, but to bless His heart. It is to bring an offering to Him that is a sweet smell, one that captivates Him. In the process of trying to capture His heart through your worship, you will find yourself head-over-heels in love with Him!

Worship causes the enemy to be scattered. We should never underestimate the power of worship to send confusion into the camp of the enemy and to cause him to flee in terror. Psalm 68:1 says "Let God arise, let his enemies be scattered…" As we lift Him up, the enemy has no choice but to run. Jehoshaphat led the Israelites in a most unusual battle strategy in 2 Chronicles 20 when he put the worshippers at the head of the army. The Bible tells us that as they began to sing and praise, their enemy became so confused that they turned on each other and began destroying one another. The Israelites never even had to lift a finger, due to the supernatural power of worship.

Worship changes atmospheres. Maybe the home in which you were raised was horrid and ungodly. Or perhaps the place you clock in every day is filled with profanity and lewdness. Or it could be that the home in which you now live is anything but a sanctuary. There is something you can do. You start by changing the atmosphere WITHIN you, which in turn will change the atmosphere AROUND you. You can't control what others do, but you can worship 24/7, anyplace, anytime.

You and God together can prevent satan from robbing you of your identity as a worshipper of the Most High. In the next chapter, we'll begin to take a look at the great value God has ascribed to you, and how the enemy seeks to steal that from you. Remember, eagles were never meant to live in chicken coops!

Chapter 5

Ahhhh.....A Masterpiece!

I joined my wife and daughter at our mini-storage unit for the arduous task of pillaging through plastic storage containers full of an assortment of items. I went kicking and screaming! A root canal or a salt-water enema seemed a more pleasurable option, but neither was available in the moment, so there I sat enduring this modern form of spousal abuse.

Okay, in all honesty, it wasn't that bad. We discovered treasures we had forgotten existed, and our stroll down memory lane caused us to stumble across some valuable works of art. Mind you, these were not old sketches from Thomas Kincaid, or a Monet painting we had discarded. These were true masterpieces, created by our children at various stages of their lives, in various settings, ranging from daycare, to school, to church, to rainy days at the kitchen table. Popsicle sticks glued together, or a tiny hand traced on construction paper can make true masterpieces worthy of any refrigerator.... or at least ours.

Funny how when you are the one creating the "masterpiece", you are so proud and think it is the greatest. Years later, you realize, as my daughter did, how simple and crude the "masterpiece" really was. But as someone has said, "Beauty is in the eye of the beholder!"

One of the most important things for people to realize is that their life is a masterpiece in the eyes of God. We find a fascinating passage of Scripture found in Deuteronomy 32:9-11. It says,

> "For the LORD's portion is his people,
> Jacob his allotted inheritance.
> 10 In a desert land he found him,
> in a barren and howling waste.
> He shielded him and cared for him;
> he guarded him as the apple of his eye,
> 11 like an eagle that stirs up its nest
> and hovers over its young,
> that spreads its wings to catch them
> and carries them on its pinions."

I hope you didn't miss it. Read it again. It says that God guards His people like the apple of His eye. Zechariah 2:8 says that "whoever touches you touches the apple of his eye." The expression "apple of his eye" refers to the pupil. It is an amazing expression in the original language that captures a concept so crucial to us protecting our identity as a masterpiece of the Lord. If anything comes near our eye, the natural reflex is to blink so that the eye is protected from the intrusion of a foreign object that could potentially damage or destroy the eye's ability to see. The pupil is the most tender part of the eye. If you look into the eyes of another person, you will see a perfect reflection of yourself in a miniature version. God sees His image in us, in a miniature version, and He watches over us to protect His image in us. A poke in the eye can be very painful, and I believe that when we allow the enemy to poke at the image of Christ in us, it is painful to the Lord. You are his masterpiece, the apple of His eye.

Our situations are all different. You may have been raised by a single mom and been called a "bastard" child all of your life. Or maybe you were raised by grandparents, or an alcoholic dad, or maybe you were abused physically or sexually. Or maybe you were fortunate enough to be raised by God-fearing parents who trained you and taught you great lessons about life. Whatever your situation, there is an enemy who seeks to steal from you the precious, high value that God places on your life.

In Ephesians 2:10, Paul writes, "For we are God's workmanship…" The New Living Translation uses the word "masterpiece" instead of "workmanship". It comes from the Greek word "poiema" which means "a work of God the creator." Imagine God as a great artist or sculptor, looking at the blank canvas of Earth. He speaks and begins to shape, create, and form mountains, sequoia trees, glaciers, rock caverns, canyons, rivers, oceans, animals, sea creatures, sunsets, stars, and galaxies. Picture him as He steps back from the canvas and a smile of satisfaction spreads across His face. The angels applaud His great work, and all that

He has just created begins to join in the applause and worship. "If you like that, then you will love this!" He says. "I have saved my best work for last. Now I will create a true masterpiece." He steps up to the canvas once again, and creates you!

You are valuable and priceless to the Lord. He created you in His image and God don't make no junk! The devil wants to try to convince you that you are nothing but yard sale material at best, but as a masterpiece of the hands of God himself, He wants to proudly display you in His collection of fine art. Sin, rebellion, lies spoken over us or other acts of evil done to us can certainly cheapen us and cloud the way we view ourselves. It is an attempt to steal your identity. But God buys us back and restores our original worth. Reminding yourself daily of the way God thinks about you, and what He has said about you, will combat the lies of the enemy.

Luke 15 records for us the story of a young man who lost his identity completely, but recaptured it again. In the next chapter, we'll look together at the process of how he lost his worth, and the steps taken to regain it.

Chapter 6

Has the devil Stolen Your Worth?

I will never forget the day I ran away from home. I had enough of my parents telling me what to do, how to dress, what to eat, where I could go, and who I could hang around. I boldly announced one morning that I was leaving, running away from home. My parents' reply was rather nonchalant, further exasperating me and pushing me out the door. So I proceeded to walk out the front door, determined never to return. I walked all the way to a large bush in the front corner of the yard, climbed inside and began acclimating myself to my new surroundings. It doesn't take long for a five year-old to start missing cartoons and snacks. I lasted all of fifteen minutes before wising up and returning home.

In Luke 15, we read the account of a young man who decides to leave home. His situation is a little different, seeing that he is a little older than five, and a little more serious about his decision. He approaches his dad and asks for his share of his father's estate. The father gives him the money, and the son leaves for what the Bible calls a distant land. Once there, he parties hard and lives it up, cruising around town on the finest two-hump camel money can buy, sporting turbans that would make any king envious. We all know that sin is fun. If that weren't the case, no one would be doing it. But it lasts only for a season, and the devil never shows us the end result until much damage is done and we are in way over our heads. And there is a progression we can follow in tracking the steps that lead to this type of identity theft. We see it in the prodigal son, and if we look closely enough, we can see it in some or many instances of our lives. Here is how it usually unfolds, and how it unfolded for him.

1. *HE WAS DEMANDING.* In Luke 15:12, we read "The younger one said to his father, "Father, give me my share of the estate." The downward spiral of destruction in a person's life begins with selfishness. We begin to act like little gods, or like the world revolves around us, and we start demanding our way. In 1 Corinthians 13:4, 5, the apostle Paul writes,

> "Love is patient and kind. Love is not jealous or boastful or proud or rude. Love does not demand its own way."

Selfishness is the opposite of the nature and heart of God, which is why the enemy wants to instill that in us. He begins the process of robbing us of our worth by causing us to focus on self more than we focus on God or others.

2. *HE BECAME DISCONNECTED.* God puts divine order into our lives. It may be your parents, your spouse, your Pastor, your boss, or all of the above. When you remove yourself from your covering, you become a target for the thief to rob you of your worth. The plan of the enemy is to isolate you, or to cause you to move yourself from the covering God put in your life. God will never allow you to be uncovered. If life's circumstances are the cause of you losing your covering (i.e. an affair on the part of your spouse that leads to divorce) God will provide a covering in some way. He will move you from one covering to another. Rebellion and sin, however, will lead you to remove yourself from the covering He put over you.

Remember this: Connection + Community = Protection. When you disconnect the plug, you lose power. Some people have unplugged themselves from the relationships that have served as a protection from the destruction of the enemy. Again we read the words of Paul in Colossians 2:18, 19 –

> "Do not let anyone who delights in false humility and the worship of angels disqualify you for the prize. Such a person goes into great detail about what he has seen, and his unspiritual mind puffs him up with idle notions. He has lost connection with the Head, from

whom the whole body, supported and held together by its ligaments and sinews, grows as God causes it to grow."

You stop growing when you become disconnected. You cannot mature spiritually outside of the Body of Christ. And you cease to function as God designed for you to function when you divorce yourself from your spiritual covering.

3. *HE WAS DESTRUCTIVE.* Luke 15:13 says that he "squandered his wealth in wild living." The KJV uses the word "wasted". This is an agricultural term that comes from the Greek word "diaskorpizo". It means "to scatter abroad, to throw the grain a considerable distance, or up into the air". The picture here is of someone taking fistfuls of money and throwing it up into the air. It is a picture of total carelessness and recklessness, of throwing caution to the wind. Proverbs 29:18 says "Where there is no revelation, the people cast off restraint…" The NLT reads this way: "When people do not accept divine guidance, they run wild."

When you disconnect yourself, you are much more likely to throw caution to the wind. The likelihood of having an affair, stealing from your employer, taking drugs, falling into the trap of pornography, or drinking becomes much greater. You lose vision and purpose when you follow the progression of focusing on self, disconnecting from your covering and from your community. Without vision and purpose, you are prone to become reckless, careless, and destructive.

People only focus on the moment, and fail to count the consequences of their destructive behavior. There are always consequences to sin, and some are more long-term than others. Again, the devil doesn't show you the end result of losing the great worth God put in you from birth. He wants you to forget that you are a masterpiece, created by the very hands of God. This leads to the next stage in the progression of having your identity stolen.

4. HE BECAME DESPERATE. Listen to the words found in Luke15:14-16 –

"After he had spent everything, there was a severe famine in that whole country, and he began to be in need. So he went and hired himself out to a citizen of that country, who sent him to his fields to feed pigs. He longed to fill his stomach with the pods that the pigs were eating, but no one gave him anything."

The devil is not satisfied with leaving you with a few scars. He wants to completely disfigure you so that you bear no resemblance whatsoever to the Father. He wants to disconnect you and lead you into such destructive behavior that you forget your origin, your birthplace, your roots, and your inheritance.

Sin will always leave you empty, and repeated disobedience will lead you to feeling worthless. Remember, you are a masterpiece that the devil wants to destroy. He is after your identity as sons and daughters of the Most High, as royal heirs to the throne and the kingship. We should all be thankful for the words found in 2 Peter 3:9, which say, "He is patient with you, not wanting anyone to perish, but everyone to come to repentance."

A powerful thing happens next in the life of the prodigal son. We can probably all relate to the words we find next in Luke 15. In verses 17 and following it says, "When he came to his senses, he said, 'How many of my father's hired men have food to spare, and here I am starving to death! I will set out and go back to my father and say to him: Father, I have sinned against heaven and against you. I am no longer worthy to be called your son; make me like one of your hired men.' So he got up and went to his father."

There comes a point of realization for all of us that the devil has stolen our worth, and that we were created for more than pig slop. The children of God were not made to live in a pig pen, just like eagles were never meant to live in a chicken coop. He was aware of his loss, and even prepared a speech to his dad that said "I am no longer worthy to be called your son." Many people have felt like that with Christ. They feel like they have fallen too far and sinned too much, to ever return as a son or daughter. But the key is found in vs. 20 – "So he got up and went to his father."

You can never recover your identity and worth until you take the first step and go home to Dad. Recovering your identity in Christ is where you find value and worth. It is not found in wealth, recognition, accomplishments, trophies, relationships, kids, degrees, houses, or titles. For worth to be restored, the item must be returned to its original state. The Father is waiting to restore you and welcome you home, not as a slave, but as a son or daughter. We also read in verse 20 – "But while he was still a long way off, his father saw him and was filled with compassion for him; he ran to his son, threw his arms around him and kissed him."

What do you have to lose? Scrape off the slop and start the trek back home to Papa. Your destiny doesn't lie in a pig pen. Remember, you are priceless, the apple of His eye, His greatest creation! He is waiting on you, and the celebration can't begin until you arrive. The devil may have been successful in stealing your worth, but God can restore you and will do as the father did in Luke 15 upon his son's return. You see, the last stage is that.......

5. HE WAS DRESSED. The father got the best robe he had and put it on his son.

And Scripture says he does the same for you and me. Isaiah 61:10 reads this way: "I delight greatly in the LORD; my soul rejoices in my God. For he has clothed me with garments of salvation and arrayed me in a **robe** of **righteousness**, as a bridegroom adorns his head like a priest, and as a bride adorns herself with her jewels."

Chapter 7

Can I Get a Witness?

When it comes to witnessing, people tend to get a little nervous. Even in a court of law you find people making some strange statements on the witness stand. Here are some examples of actual statements that people have made while testifying in court.[1]

Q: What is your date of birth?
A: July fifteenth.
Q: What year?
A: Every year.

Q: Sir, what is your IQ?
A: Well, I can see pretty well, I think.

Q:Now doctor, isn't it true that when a person dies in his sleep, he doesn't know anything about it until the morning?

Q: She had three children, right?
A: Yes.
Q: How many were boys?
A: None.
Q: Were there any girls?

Q: How old is your son-the one living with you?
A: Thirty-eight or thirty-five, I can't remember which.
Q: How long has he lived with you?
A: Forty-five years.

Q: You were there until the time you left, is that true?

Q: You were not shot in the fracas?
A: No, I was shot midway between the fracas and the navel.

A person is called to the witness stand in court to testify about the events they have witnessed. They are sworn to tell the truth, and thus they then become a declaration of facts. They are not called to prove anything but simply to declare the facts. Often times when we think of witnessing for Christ, we shift into panic mode. If placed in a situation where we are compelled to share Christ with someone, our palms begin to clam up, our throat becomes as dry as the desert floor, and our voice takes on a higher pitch mixed with erratic quivering. It can be an ugly scene. Most people have some grave misunderstandings about witnessing, which the devil loves. The top three reasons people do not share their faith or witness are:

1. Fear
2. Fear
3. Fear

Most Christians in America, then, choose to "leave that for those who are called to do it." And God is left saying, "Can I get a witness?"

It may help to understand a few truths about witnessing.

Truth 1: Witnessing is not necessarily preaching. You don't have to have 200 scriptures memorized, have a degree in theology from a school of divinity, or even know the Romans Road. Paul makes this statement in 1 Corinthians 2:4 – "… and so nothing I said could have impressed you or anyone else. But the Message came through anyway." (from THE MESSAGE: The Bible in Contemporary Language © 2002 by Eugene H. Peterson. All rights reserved.)

Truth 2: Witnessing does not have to be confrontational. So often, we have it in our minds that if we ever do step out and share our faith with someone, it is going to look like a UFC battle in the Octagon. We envision there being yelling and violence, or at best, red faces and clenched fists. Although the Gospel is confrontational, witnessing doesn't have to be. I am thankful that everyday I am confronted by the truth of God's

Word. It keeps me on a path of righteousness. But truth spoken without love will harden a heart. Truth spoken with love can lead to a turning towards the Lord. Remember, Romans 2:4 says "God's kindness leads you toward repentance."

Truth 3: Witnessing can be verbal or non-verbal. A large part of communication is non-verbal. Some of your greatest statements will be made without ever saying a word. A popular quote came years ago from St. Francis of Assisi: "Preach the Gospel everyday....when necessary, use words."

Truth 4: Witnessing is not proving anything, but just declaring facts. Debating scripture is never the goal of sharing your faith. There is a place for apologetics, and we need to study in order to rightly divide the word of truth. But it is not our responsibility to prove anything. A witness in court does not bear the burden of proof, but only to speak of what he or she knows to be fact based on what was seen or experienced. Everyone has a story to tell, and once you accept Christ as Messiah and Lord of your life, you can speak of your life before Christ, tell what brought you to the place of asking Christ to come inside and transform you, and what your life is like since. No one can tell your story better than you!

Truth 5: Witnessing is not optional. Every believer is called upon to speak of what they know to be factual based on what has been seen or experienced. This can be done in a variety of ways, but it is a non-negotiable for the believer. Scripture does not encourage us to witness, but commands us to witness.

If Christ lives in you, then you are a person of influence. His very presence in you spills over in your actions, your words, and your lifestyle, and affects the way others live. When your life bears witness to the fact that Christ is alive, you then become a declaration of truth that upsets the powers of hell. You are witnessing as to who He is, and reflecting His image like a mirror so others can see Him through you.

Your relationship with Christ should be the most exciting, energizing, wonderful experience of your life. If that is not true, then chances are you are just caught up in religion, not a relationship. There is no romance, no relationship that compares to a relationship with Christ, and speaking about that should be a natural outflow of our lives. Matthew 12:34 says, "For out of the overflow of the heart the mouth speaks."

Unfortunately, many believers have allowed the fear of man, or the intimidation of past failures and mistakes, to silence their witness, or to do what we find a man in the Bible doing. In the following chapter, we'll look at Jonah's actions, and how we can recover our identity as faithful witnesses for Christ.

[1] From the book "Disorder in the Court"

Chapter 8

Run, Jonah, Run!

In Jonah 1:1-3 we find this story recorded:

"The word of the LORD came to Jonah son of Amittai: 2 "Go to the great city of Nineveh and preach against it, because its wickedness has come up before me." 3But Jonah ran away from the LORD and headed for Tarshish. He went down to Joppa, where he found a ship bound for that port. After paying the fare, he went aboard and sailed for Tarshish to flee from the LORD."

Let's not be too quick to judge Jonah or be too hard on the guy. We have all been there. We can all relate. Jonah heard clearly from the Lord but decided to do the opposite of what he heard. God gave him a tough assignment, no doubt. Nineveh was a large, important city in Assyria, located along the Tigris River. It posed a strong military threat to Israel, and had a reputation of being ruthless and bloodthirsty. In fact, the Assyrians themselves left monuments to their cruelty. These monuments contained long, boastful inscriptions describing their torture and slaughter of people who opposed them. Imagine jumping into a crowd of cage fighters and calling them all sissies. Or showing up at the mall the day after Thanksgiving and telling everyone in line that they are all materialistic hedonists! These two things would be a cakewalk compared to what God was calling Jonah to do.

God wanted Jonah to travel to Nineveh to declare the truth about their iniquity. Jonah probably pictured an effigy of himself in the center of Nineveh with the words "Not in our town!" written beneath. Keep in mind that when God taps us for an assignment, He has already seen in us the qualifications needed to complete the assignment. He knew Jonah was capable, but because of identity theft, Jonah did not see himself as God saw him. Gideon was the same way in Judges 6. The Midianites were out to destroy the Israelites, everyone was hiding in caves, trembling with fear, and Gideon was tucked away in a valley hoping to stay below the radar. God found him, however, tapped him to declare the truth, and called him a mighty warrior. God saw him for who he really was and for the potential for greatness that lay within.

And He sees the same in you and me. We were created to witness, and included in our spiritual DNA is the ability to declare the facts, the truth of our love relationship with Christ. Unfortunately, Jonah chose to do what many of us have done......HE RAN! Funny how quickly we can forget that "if God be for us, who can be against us?" Again, we are all prone to cave in from time to time. And we can learn how to recover, how to prevent a permanent loss of identity, from Jonah. We see from the story in Scripture that Jonah took some simple steps to regain what was lost. You can do the same.

First, ***call to Him***. Mistakes can humble you, or you can respond with pride. Cry out to Him immediately. The longer you wait, the more difficult it becomes to call to Him. Jonah 2:1 says "In my distress I called to the Lord, and he answered me." If someone began using your credit card, posing as you, as a result of a mistake you made, you would still call the authorities and report it. When you lose your witness as a result of something you have done, the best thing you can do is immediately call to the Lord.

Second, ***confess your mistake***. David is the only one in the Bible of whom it was said that he was a man after God's own heart. It was said not once, but twice. David lost his witness when he committed adultery with Bathsheba. He wrote his confession for all to read, and owned up to his mistake in Psalm 51:3, 4, "For I know my transgressions, and my sin is always before me. 4 Against you, you only, have I sinned and done what is evil in your sight…" Confession releases the presence of God in your life, which then drives out sin, pride, shame, and anything else that is contrary to the image of Christ. In 1 John 1:9 we read, "If we confess our sins, he is faithful and just and will forgive us our sins and purify us from all unrighteousness."

Third, ***commit yourself***. Jonah said in vs. 9, "What I have vowed, I will make good." When God restores our identity and our witness, it is not only for future encounters, but it is also for the sake of going back and making good on a missed opportunity, if possible. One of my favorite scriptures in the Bible is found in Jonah 3:1, "Then the word of the Lord came to Jonah a second time." What a picture of the patience and mercy of the Lord. When we miss an opportunity to declare the facts, to witness and speak about who He is, it is important that we learn from the missed opportunity so that we don't repeat the mistake. This will also give you a keener sense of hearing the prophetic voice of the Lord in future situations. And God is faithful to speak again. Joy for him does not come from rubbing our noses in the messes we make, but rather from watching us learn, mature, grow, and obey when He does speak again.

I believe Eugene Robinson brought the Lord joy—not because of the mistake that caused him to lose his identity as a witness for Christ, but because of how he responded. It was Saturday morning, January 30th, 1999, just one day before Super Bowl XXXIII. Eugene Robinson, the 14-year all-pro safety for the Atlanta Falcons, was named the 1999 winner of the Bart Starr Award by Athletes in Action, an award that traditionally honors high moral character. Robinson was known for his strong walk with Christ, and had the respect of teammates, opposing players, and fans.

An enemy was lurking, however, determined to rob him of his identity and his testimony. Around

9:00PM that evening, the football great was on the receiving end of a devastating blow when he was arrested in a seedy area of Miami for soliciting a prostitute. The media had a field day and Robinson suffered great embarrassment and humiliation. He spent some five hours praying during a sleepless night, crying out to God and recovering his lost identity.

The Falcons did not win the Super Bowl that year, but Eugene Robinson gained something much more valuable than a Super Bowl ring. He gained the value of his identity as a witness for Christ. He called out to the Lord, he confessed his mistake, and he committed himself to being the man of God, husband, and father God created him to be. Eugene Robinson never belonged in that part of Miami, just like eagles don't belong in chicken coops.

Chapter 9

Has the devil Stolen Your Wealth?

"We've been robbed!" were the words I heard from the young lady working the drive-thru window of a fast-food restaurant. I was at the counter getting ready to place my order when a car pulled up to the window, the driver flashed a gun, demanded money, and sped off. It happens every day to believers. The devil borrows the line from a popular movie and says, "Show me the money!" and in a flash snatches wealth from the hands of believers. John 10:10 gives us a clear warning that "the thief comes to steal…."

Raising my children is expensive. I have thought about keeping a running tab of all the expenses associated with their upbringing, and then after they turn eighteen, setting up a billing plan for them to repay the money. It might take them until they hit retirement age to pay it all off, but at least I could get my money back. Of course, when I die it is all going to them anyway, so I figured it would sort of be a wash. Not to mention the fact that it wouldn't be very Christ-like. "Show me the money, kids!" Easy.... I'm kidding!

Having been created in the image of God means that it is in our nature to give. John 3:16 tells us that God loved the world and therefore He gave. I actually enjoy giving to my children and find great joy in blessing them and doing things for them. When we give we experience life. A pond with no outlet will eventually stagnate and stink. So will our lives. God designed us to be givers. Selfishness is the opposite of the character and nature of God. It is the plan and goal of the enemy to cause us to become selfish with our time, our talent, and our treasure. This brings death, not life, which is really his ultimate goal. So the devil's attempt to rob you of your wealth is an attempt to keep you from functioning in the image and likeness of God, which is to give.

Some people freak out when Christians talk about money, but the fact is that Jesus spoke more about money than he did about heaven or hell. The money God puts into our hands can represent influence that will expand the kingdom of God if we protect it from the enemy, and if we allow ourselves to function in our Dad's likeness. And just what is that? Scripture draws us an accurate portrait with words like this.....

"He owns the cattle on a thousand hills."

"The earth is the Lord's and all it contains."

He is El-shaddai – El – "God", shad – "breast". This refers to God completely nourishing, satisfying, and supplying His people with all their needs as a mother would her child. Connected with the word for God, *El*, this denotes a God who freely gives nourishment and blessing. He is the God of more than enough, the God who gives power to gain wealth, and the God who supplies needs.

The Israelites made a very costly mistake by not guarding their wealth. In 1 Kings 14:25-27 we find these words: "In the fifth year of King Rehoboam, Shishak king of Egypt attacked Jerusalem. 26 He carried off the treasures of the temple of the LORD and the treasures of the royal palace. He took everything, including all the gold shields Solomon had made. 27 So King Rehoboam made bronze shields to replace them and assigned these to the commanders of the guard on duty at the entrance to the royal palace."

There are three powerful truths that stand out about this story. Notice this…… **no one was guarding the gold.** In our story, Shishak invaded Jerusalem and he took everything. For whatever reason, they had become careless and were not watching over the treasures. Thirty five miles south of Louisville, KY is a place known as Fort Knox. It is an 110,000 acre post that houses the US gold depository. It is guarded by more than just a pit bull and a chain link fence.

How many times do we become careless in our lives, not just with money, but with other treasures like our marriage, our future, our salvation, our children, our friendships, and not put sufficient guards in place to protect those things that are valuable to us? Again, we read in John 10:10, "The thief comes only to steal and kill and destroy..." The devil wants to take everything from you. He wants to plunder you to the point that you bear no resemblance to your Father. When you are robbed of your wealth, you lose the resemblance of the one in whose image you were created. You are not just guarding your money, possessions, relationships, and other treasures. You are actually guarding the image of God inside of you.

Secondly, I want you to see that **brass can never replace gold.**

In vs. 27, we read, "So King Rehoboam made bronze shields to replace them and assigned these to the commanders of the guard on duty at the entrance to the royal palace." You can shine it, buff it, polish it, or paint it, but it will never be gold. It is a sad thing to see someone who once had the gold, but didn't value it enough to protect it and guard it. When we lose it because of rebellion or negligence, in most cases you don't get the opportunity to get it back. God is a restorer, and He is in the business of helping us to get back on our feet and to recover our identity in Him. But the things that we lose are often lost forever. Can we be used again? Married again? Blessed again? Of course. But it may not be the gold you had in the beginning.

Lastly, we need to realize that, unfortunately for some, **it takes losing the gold to appreciate the brass.** Don't ever believe the sales pitch of the devil that the brass will one day turn to gold. Brass is better than having nothing, but it is not as good as the gold and it will not magically turn to gold.

Those who have lost the gold often have a great appreciation for the brass. Verse 28 says, "Whenever the king went to the Lord's temple, the guards bore the shields, and afterward they returned them to the guardroom." They were not careless anymore. Now they put guards around the shields. Why didn't they do that before? It is a classic example of the old saying that "you never know what you had until it is gone."

Learning to protect our identity as givers and rightful heirs to the blessings and provisions of the Lord comes with gaining a greater understanding of the purposes of the resources God entrusts to us. We'll talk about that in the next chapter as we continue in the journey of recovering stolen identities.

Chapter 10

Pour, Prime, Pump, and Prosper

The following letter was found in a baking-powder can wired to the handle of an old pump that offered the only hope of drinking water on a very long and seldom-used trail across Nevada's Amargosa Desert: "This pump is all right as of June 1932. I put a new sucker washer into it and it ought to last five years. But the washer dries out and the pump has got to be primed. Under the white rock I buried a bottle of water, out of the sun and cork end up. There's enough water in it to prime the pump, but not if you drink some first. Pour about one-fourth and let her soak to wet the leather. Then pour in the rest medium fast and pump like crazy. You'll git water. The well has never run dry. Have faith. When you git watered up, fill the bottle and put it back like you found it for the next feller. (signed) Desert Pete. P.S.

Don't go drinking the water first. Prime the pump with it and you'll git all you can hold."

'Ole Desert Pete hit on something that is so key for us when it comes to the way we view and handle wealth and resources. If we follow biblical principles and have faith, we will be blessed with more than enough. The tough part for most of us is that there is always a temptation to satisfy ourselves first, to take care of our own needs before we can think about taking care of someone else's needs. Reaping will always follow sowing. It is a law, just like the law of gravity, that doesn't accommodate our belief system. There are four principles about reaping that are important for us to understand.

1. You reap **if** you sow. It is as simple as that. We have the choice of whether or not we will sow.
2. You reap **what** you sow. If a farmer plants corn, he doesn't scratch his head wondering why wheat didn't come up. If you sow kindness, time, patience, money, or anything else, that is what you will reap.
3. You reap **more than** you sow. The disciples were faced with a tough decision when Jesus handed them five loaves of bread and a couple of fish, after He blessed it, and told them to begin handing it out to over 12,000 people. But as they obeyed and began sowing, the miracle occurred while they were distributing it. Everyone was fed, and there were 12 baskets of leftovers.
4. You reap **how** you sow. Paul writes in Galatians 9:6, "Whoever sows sparingly will also reap

sparingly, and whoever sows generously will also reap generously."

In his book The Blessed Life, Pastor Robert Morris shares some truths about how we should view the resources God has put into our hands. Your treasures can be viewed by you in 3 ways. First of all, we can view them through the lenses of NEED. This mentality says that we get money solely to meet our needs. Secondly, we can view resources through the lenses of GREED. This is the level above need, or sufficiency, and it is where we are all tested. It is the level of abundance, and the mentality at this level is that I have been blessed to not only meet my needs, but to fulfill my desires. The third and most fulfilling and powerful way to view our resources are as SEED. This level represents the highest use of money. The mentality at this level says, "I've been blessed in order to be a blessing, to sow seed, to give it away, in order to get more so that I can give more." In 2 Corinthians 9:10,11, Paul writes, "Now he who supplies seed to the sower and bread for food will also supply and increase your store of seed and will enlarge the harvest of your righteousness. [11]You will be made rich in every way so that you can be generous on every occasion…" Notice that it does not say "God supplies seed to the keeper", but seed to the sower. In Ecclesiastes 11:1, it says "Cast your bread upon the waters, for after many days you will find it again."

People say things like this: "Someday, when I have more money (time), I'm going to be a giver." It will never happen. You cannot reap before you sow. It is a divine order that God established. Imagine a farmer standing in a field looking for a crop to come up, even though he never planted a seed. Or what if he said, "I'll have a lot more seed to sow whenever this crop finally comes in." One of the kingdom principles taught and established by Jesus is that you start where you are, with what you have. The one who is faithful with little will receive much! If you can't tithe on $100, what makes you think you will tithe on $1 million?

David gives us a vivid image of the sower and of the joy that accompanies the sacrificial act of sowing when he writes these words:

> Ps. 126:5, 6 – "Those who sow in tears
> will reap with songs of joy.
> [6] He who goes out weeping,
> carrying seed to sow,
> will return with songs of joy,
> carrying sheaves with him."

Philip Cameron is a missionary evangelist with a heart for the country of Moldova. While speaking at The Refuge, he shared how the government had signed over to him the largest orphanage in the country, one that houses 650 children. The windows all needed to be replaced and it was going to cost $170,000. We took an offering that day and sowed over $7000 into the project. During this time, The Refuge, after searching for over a year, put a building under contract and launched into a capital campaign to raise funds. I kept sensing the Lord whispering in my spirit that He was going to require us to sow a significant seed at a time that we most needed the money. For some reason, I had in my mind that it would be $50,000.

A few months later, I received a phone call from a local business man who shared with me that God had spoken to his heart and wanted him to sow $100,000 into missions IF The Refuge would match it. I immediately knew that God was at work. This man felt impressed of the Lord to sow $100,000 toward the purchase of the windows in Moldova. We decided to give the remaining $70,000 to the project in Moldova, and the other $30,000 to another project of The Refuge in Brazil.

Two weeks later I was with Philip for some meetings. The checks had not yet been sent, but I pulled him aside and told him what was about to happen. He was completely shocked, and then shared with me that just two days earlier, he had gathered his staff together and informed them that he had apparently missed God on the orphanage. The money was not coming in, and for the first time ever, he was going to have to abandon a project he had committed to complete. This of course was disheartening to this man of vision and faith, and he knew that it would jeopardize, and possibly destroy, the favor he had found with the government officials in Moldova.

But God had a plan in the works, and it involved people and a community of believers operating in the image and likeness of their Father, pouring out and sowing generously for the sake of the Kingdom.

Chapter 11

Can I Raise My Credit Score?

God's purposes and plans for you have been established long before you existed. And they are wonderful, complete, exciting plans. In Jeremiah 29:11 it says "For I know the plans I have for you," declares the LORD, "plans to prosper you and not to harm you, plans to give you hope and a future." But the enemy also has a plan for you, one that involves humiliation, frustration, guilt, failure, poverty, and death. Jealous of the resemblance you bear to the Father, he sets traps to lure you into a life of compromise and disobedience, chiseling away at the countenance of the Most High that was put in you from the beginning.

One of the many negative consequences to identity theft in our society is the damage to one's credit score. Many advertisements and commercials now focus on how you can raise or rebuild your credit score. These ads have people wondering how they compare to others. One ad even depicts a low credit score that is attached to a man and is visible to everyone, causing him much embarrassment.

Many victims of spiritual identity theft carry around the shame of selling out, losing identity, compromising, or failing. There is a misconception that somehow you must raise your credit score before you can ever qualify for God's favor or forgiveness again. You feel the pressure to "get it all together" before approaching God and endeavoring to recapture your identity in Him.

Receiving God's grace and forgiveness is not dependant on your spiritual credit score. You cannot work enough, give enough, or do enough to merit it. The Holy Spirit may have stirred your heart throughout the pages of this book, bringing you to this point and to a place that you are desperate and determined to once again look like the One who created you. Maybe you have realized that you are a victim, you fell for the scam, and the devil succeeded in robbing you of your worship, your worth, your witness, or your wealth.

If that is the case, stop right now and pray this out loud:

"Jesus, I have come to a point of realization. I realize that I have lost my identity as one created in your image. I realize that I have made choices that have caused me to lose the resemblance I once bore to your face, your heart, and to your character. And I am reminded that you created me as a masterpiece, as the apple of your eye, and that you still love me today. I run to you today, Dad. I confess my sins, my mistakes, my failures and I throw myself at the mercy of your love, trusting the power of your blood to forgive, to wash, to purify, and to restore. I turn my back on habits, relationships, activities, and thoughts that are in opposition to your nature. I want to recapture my identity in you as one created in your image. I surrender my past, my present, and my future to you today. In Jesus' name, amen."

Now, the past is behind you, and your destiny awaits you! Having prayed that prayer with sincerity, trust now in the power of His blood to wash you and make you new. Revelation 12:11 tells us that "They overcame him by the blood of the Lamb and by the word of their testimony." The ingredient other than His blood that will enable you to walk and remain in His image is your words. Speaking truth contradicts and neutralizes the power of the devil's lies. The truth now is that you are clean, forgiven, restored, and ready to walk in stride with your Father. So establish that truth everyday by speaking of what God has done and who you are in Him. This is important whether you are a new believer or a seasoned warrior. Brag on Jesus to anyone who will listen, and if you are unable to find anyone to tell, just speak it into the atmosphere. There is great power in your testimony.

While walking through the forest one day, a man found a young eagle that had fallen out of his nest. He took it home and put it in his barnyard where it soon learned to eat and behave like the chickens. One day a naturalist passed by the farm and asked why it was that the king of all birds should be confined to live in the barnyard with the chickens. The farmer replied that since he had given it chicken feed and trained it to be a chicken, it had never learned to fly. Since it now behaved as the chickens, it was no longer an eagle.

"Still it has the heart of an eagle," replied the naturalist, "and can surely be taught to fly." He lifted the eagle toward the sky and said, "You belong to the sky and not to the earth. Stretch forth your wings and fly." The eagle, however, was confused. He did not know who he was, and seeing the chickens eating their food, he jumped down to be with them again.

The naturalist took the bird to the roof of the house and urged him again, saying, "You are an eagle. Stretch forth your wings and fly." But the eagle was afraid of his unknown self and world and jumped down once more for the chicken food. Finally the naturalist took the eagle out of the barnyard to a high mountain. There he held the king of the birds high above him and encouraged him again, saying, "You are an eagle. You belong to the sky. Stretch forth your wings and fly." The eagle looked around, back towards the barnyard and up to the sky. Then the naturalist lifted him straight towards the sun and it happened that the eagle began to tremble. Slowly he stretched his wings, and with a triumphant cry, soared away into the heavens.

Now is your time to fly.......so mount up with wings of eagles and soar as the Son or Daughter of God you are! It may be scary at first, but point your face towards the Son, refuse to look back at the past, and go for it. You are an eagle, and eagles don't belong in chicken coops!

Printed in the United States
200060BV00003B/1-393/A